THIS BOOK WAS WRITTEN IN TWO THOUSAND THIRTEEN BY CALANDRA IZQUIERDO & LAZARUS POTTER. IT IS SET IN THE TYPEFACES NOVEL, VLADIMIR SCRIPT, AND EFFECT REGULAR. LAYOUT & DESIGN BY ALLISON MULLER.

Welcome

People are driven to communicate with any tools at hand. From cave paintings to the worldwide internet, we can, and will send messages.

In this book we take a look at texting and text etiquette.

Texting came out of the two-way pager technology of the 80's. You could send messages that revealed their meaning only after you turned your pager upside down. Do you remember your first 01134 or 58008?

With over 6.2 billion active phones in the world and advancements like T9-Predictive, SWYPE and full keyboards, it is easier than ever for people to have their entire relationship in text messages.

"I fear the day when technology
overlaps our humanity. It will
be then that the world will have
permanent ensuing
generations of idiots."

-Albert Einstein

Has this texting technology brought people closer together? Have the 5.9 trillion texts sent a year helped our understanding of each other and our interpersonal relations?

With do's and do nots of texting etiquette, text messaging can be a useful tool.

We have noticed that some people are abusing, and losing, much needed relationship skills.

We are here to help.

Welcome to Textiquette.

Fact

SMS stands for
Short Message Service

DO NOT

text a book.
TEXT IS USED AS
a message,
NOT A CONVERSATION.
CALL THE PERSON.

DO NOT

text while driving.
if you're being told this
YOU PROBABLY
SHOULDN'T BE DRIVING
TO BEGIN WITH.
ARRIVE ALIVE

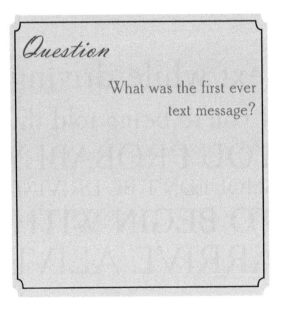

Question

What was the first ever
text message?

DO NOT

text again if a
TEXT IS NOT ANSWERED
RIGHT AWAY,
the recipient is busy.
THEY WILL GET BACK TO
YOU WHEN THEY CAN.

Answer

"Happy Christmas" December 8, 1992. Sent by Neil Papworth who texted Vodafone director Richard Jarvis at a staff Christmas party.

DO

respond to all LEGITIMATE TEXTS.

(this does not include texts from an ex)

DO NOT

text during a
DOCTOR'S
APPOINTMENT
being healthy is more
important than
SUSAN'S SHOES.

Fact

The first text message phone -
the Orbitel mobile phone.

DO

include your name
AND WHERE YOU MET
on the first text with
SOMEONE NEW.

Fact

1920 - RCA Communications
introduced the first "telex"
service. The first messages over
transatlantic circuits were sent
between New York and London.
300,000 radiograms were
transmitted the first year.
RCA today is known
as Verizon Wireless.

DO NOT

send an informational
TEXT AT 2AM.
while on the subject of 2am, don't send
ANY TEXT AT THAT TIME,
if it's an emergency
DIAL 911.

Why are text messages limited
to 160 characters?

DO NOT

text
WHILE ON
A DATE.

Friedhelm Hillebrand, a member
of the group defining SMS,
set out to figure out how many
characters you needed to ask a
question. He used a typewriter
and he decided that 160
characters was enough to write a
sentence or ask a question.

DO

turn your phone
OFF AT A
MOVIE THEATER.

Fact

Nokia, in 1993, was the first mobile phone which allowed people to send text messages.

DO NOT

make up
YOUR OWN
ABBREVIATIONS.

Fact

The IBM Simon was the first touchscreen phone in 1992. It is also referred to as the first "smartphone."

DO

use proper
GRAMMAR
and
SPELL CHECK

anidifnotmaybbushldttext.

(and if not maybe you shouldn't text)

What was the first phone with
a keyboard?

DO NOT

be late
BECAUSE YOU ARE
CHARGING YOUR
cellphone.

The Nokia 9000i Communicator.
In 1997, Nokia became the first
manufacturer to produce a mobile
phone with a full keyboard.

DO NOT

EVER
BREAKUP
through a text
or because of one.

What does T-9 stand for?

DO

use text as a
QUICK FORM
OF
COMMUNICATION
"be there in 5"
"SEE YOU @ 2PM"

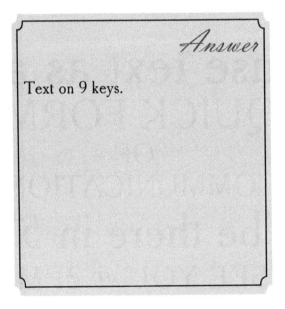

Answer

Text on 9 keys.

DO NOT

read a text message
WHILE HAVING A
CONVERSATION
with someone.
IT IS RUDE AND
THEY DESERVE YOUR
attention
AND
respect.

In the 1990s, Cliff Kushler invented T9. Instead of multi-tapping, predictive text technology displays words from a single keypress. As the texter uses T9 it learns your words and phrases, making texting faster.

DO NOT

text while
CHECKING OUT
in a store
or ordering a drink
at the bar.

In 2011, Kushler invented Swype,
a texting feature for touchscreens
that enables users to drag their
fingers to connect the dots between
letters in a word.

DO NOT

feel you always need
TO RESPOND TO
EVERY
BEEP
your phone makes.
HAVE SOME CLASS
when in public.

Fact

Sexting is slang for the act of sending sexually explicit or suggestive content between mobile devices using SMS.

DO NOT

send "did i fuck up?" text.
DO YOU REALLY WANT TO KNOW?
YOU PROBABLY KNOW THE ANSWER.
start thinking of ways to
make it up to
THAT PERSON.

Fact

The iPhone was introduced June 29th 2007 by Apple.

DO NOT

use a text to ask
someone out
ON A DATE.
if you want to
IMPRESS SOMEONE
MAKE IT
PERSONAL.

DO

TURN YOUR PHONE
OFF AT
BAND PRACTICE.
music makes the world
a better place, and
YOU NEED TO
PRACTICE.

Fact

Remember The Old Nokia Text
Message Tone?
It's Morse Code For 'SMS'...

DO NOT

interpret emotion
through text.
PICK UP THE PHONE
AND CALL
or better yet
KNOCK ON THEIR DOOR.

1999 was the first year that you could text someone on a different phone provider.

DO NOT

drunk text.
NO, NO, NO
INTEXTIGATING.

There were more than 8 trillion
text messages sent worldwide
in 2011.

DO

send random texts
OF KINDNESS,
it always puts a
SMILE ON FACES.

Fact

In 2011, LOL was added to the Oxford dictionary.

DO NOT

text confidential
INFORMATION.

Fact

Brennan Hayden sent the first paid-for commercial text in June 1993. Hayden sent the word "burp" because he saw the medium as a new baby.

DO

text to
CONFIRM
PLANS.

The razor-toothed piranhas of the genera Serrasalmus and Pygocentrus are the most ferocious freshwater fish in the world. In reality they seldom attack a human.

This is the sentence used by Guinness World Records to measure speed texting.

DO NOT

text in TRAFFIC.

Fact

The first Android powered
phone was sold
in October 2008.

DO NOT

text while
CROSSING
THE STREET.
if you're walking and texting,
BE AWARE
of other pedestrians.

DO NOT

text during
A MEETING.

Fact

79% of people have admitted
to text messaging while using
the bathroom.

DO

turn your phone
OFF
DURING A JOB
interview.

DO NOT

put your phone
ON THE
DINNER TABLE.

Fact

Text messages are usually
read within 15 minutes of
being received and responded
to within one hour.

DO NOT

text
IN THE
SHOWER.

In Closing

g2g, ttyl

Please see our glossary to decipher the above message.

DO NOT

get caught up
on text messaging.
THE WORLD WILL BE A
HAPPIER PLACE
when we all know
WHEN TO
TEXT AND WHEN TO TALK.
LIFE
IS WHAT HAPPENS
WHEN YOU'RE NOT TEXTING.

So, that is what we think.

What do you think? We invite you to join
our on-going discussion on the Do's and Do
Nots of Texting at **clever**
OR
NOT
dot com

Please join us, send in your textiquettes,
add to our glossary, share your DO's and
share your DO NOTs.

Need to send us a text: (816) 200-2834
we would love to hear from you.

Coming Soon
The Amazing Misguided Adventures of
Facebook Relationships. (Lots of DO
NOTs there)

Peace, Love, Harmony

Glossary

ABT	About	EZ	Easy
ADDY	Address	F	Female
AH	At Home	F2F	Face To Face
AIR	As I Remember	FAB	Fabulous
ASAP	As Soon As Possible	FAQ	Frequently Asked Questions
B2W	Back To Work	FB	Facebook
B4	Before	FML	F* My Life
B4N	Before Now	FTFU	Fixed That For You
B4U	Before You	FTW	For The Win!
B8	Bait	FW	Forward
BC	Because	FWIW	For What It's Worth
BDAY	Birthday	FYEO	For Your Eyes Only
BEG	Big Evil Grin	FYI	For Your Information
BF	Boyfriend	G1	Good One
BFF	Best Friend Forever	G2CU	Good To See You
BKA	Better Known As	G2G	Got to go
BRB	Be Right Back	G4C	Going For Coffee
BTW	By The Way	GB	Goodbye
BYOB	Bring Your Own Beer	GBTW	Get Back To Work
BZ	Busy	GBU	God Bless You
CM	Call Me	GF	Girlfriend
CMB	Call Me Back	GOL	Giggling Out Loud
CRAY-CRAY	Crazy to a new level	GR8	Great
CRAFT	Can't Remember A F*ing Thing	GRATZ	Congratulations
		GTFOH	Get the F* Outta Here
CU	See You	H	Hug
DITTO	Same Here	H&K	Hugs & Kisses
DND	Do Not Disturb	H8	Hate
DWBH	Don't Worry Be Happy	HAU	How About You
E1	Everyone	HBD	Happy Birthday
ENUF	Enough	HMU	Hit Me Up
EOD	End Of Day	HTFU	Harden The F* Up
ETA	Estimated Time Of Arrival	HW	Homework
		IC	I See